To College or Not to College©

Casey Bell

ISBN: 978-0-692-89154-4

Cover Design by Casey Bell

Printed in the United States

Casey Bell
PO Box 5231
Old Bridge, NJ 08857

authorcaseybell.com

lulu.com/spotlight/motownbg

CONTENTS

TO COLLEGE OR NOT TO COLLEGE POEM

To College or Not to College that is the question

To be educated in debt or to self-educate for free

To trade, militate, or entrepreneut

To invent, create, or to compute

To buy expensive college books or to take out free library books

To College or Not to College which do I choose?

Do I be a paper cut out and follow suit?

Or do I follow my fingerprints and be unique?

Which is best for me, the paved pathway or the unpaved way which I pave?

To College or Not to College should I choose the most popular?

Or do I do what is best for me?

Whether it be vocational, trade, college, or self

Which education is best for me?

To College or Not to College is education really expensive?

Or are their choices of cheap, expensive, or free?

To College or Not to College that is the question for me.

Which will I choose?

INTRODUCTION

To College or not to college that is the question. In today's times (2016) America is making a big deal about college as if it is the only choice in becoming a successful person or successful at life. You are a completely wrong if you believe that because there are thousands even millions of successful people in America who do not have a college degree. Most of them are more successful than those who have a college degree. We have evidence and results that you can be successful without going to college and yet we still lie and say college is your only answer to success. The other lie Americans tell is the following: "Education is expensive." That is a lie. College is expensive, not education. College is one option of being educated, but not the only option and is not the best option. In this book you will find out the truth and facts about who needs college and for those who do not need it your options. The options your teachers, pastors, parents, and your government either refuse to tell you or just do not know to tell you. But that's okay that's why I am writing this book to show readers their options. This book is divided into three sections: "To College" reveals who needs college and ways to save money in the process of going to college. The second section is "Not to College", which gives you your many options of being educated so you can be just as successful (if not more) as those who are in college. And finally the last section is the conclusion. I hope you read this with an open mind. Before we start there is something you need to know (something most people in the world do not know). I do not care what is in your life (bad things) there is always at least two options (if not more) to solve the problem. If your doctor says surgery is the only answer do your research. Your doctor says that because surgery is the only option for him to make enough money to pay for his mansion or luxury car, but it is not the only option for you. If your pastor, teacher, professor, car salesperson, whoever tells you, you only have one choice do your research. They are lying to you (either knowingly or unknowingly). There are always two or more choices you just have to search and find it. So as you read this book takes notes and make sure you do lots of research after reading it to find not only the options in this book, but to see if you can find more. Options to anything in life are like Waldo or words in a search puzzle. They are there, you may find them immediately, or it may take some time, but just because you don't find it doesn't mean it's not there it just means you didn't search hard enough. Keep searching until you find your options.

TO COLLEGE

There are a few professions where having a college degree is required by law. Any field in the medical fields (doctor, nurse, etc), teachers, professors, lawyers, psychologist, certain counseling fields, and many others. If you are aware of what you want to do with your life research and see if you are required a degree. If the answer is yes, unless you want to be in prison than go to college. For those who realize no law states they need a degree than go to the second section, if you do not find another option you want to take than come back to section one.

So you're going to college. For some of you it's an option for others it's the law. Either or, there are many options that are not given to you as far as college goes. Before we talk about choosing a college and degree let's first discuss payment. I am not sure why, but Americans make a huge deal about college, but don't prepare for it. If you know you want your child to go to college, than why don't you financially prepare for it? That is not smart. So let's talk financial preparation. There are many options you need to know about.

TO THE PARENTS

Once you know for sure you want to have children (even if you are childless) that is the time to start preparing for college. Open a savings account and never touch it. The good thing about it is if you do not have children or they choose not to go to college (because they read section two of this book) then at least you have money on the side for whatever you want. There are many different accounts you can open (That you do NOT touch): Savings Bonds, CDs, Money Market Mutual Funds, US Treasury Bills, US Treasury Notes, Treasury Bonds, Stock Mutual Funds, and many more (Do your research.) The main thing is DO not touch it. Just make deposits at least once a week, $100, $10, $1, or even $0.01, but make sure you are making deposits on the regular. Now let's say you just got pregnant, start the account. Well the child is three years old, than start the account. Do not wait until they are 17 to start thinking about money for college. Even when they are just a tinkle in your eye start saving. The good thing about this account there is no law that says you have to use it for college. This way if your child ends up on a free ride to college (scholarships) than you have extra money for either your retirement or a vacation. There are also saving accounts you can start by different companies that are specifically for college only (Do your research on that.) Ask your bank or credit union (credit unions are better than banks (do your research)) for information on which account is better for you. Ask all questions smart and dumb. Here are few websites to get you started:

savingforcollege.com   collegesavings.org

gerberlife.com   upromise.com

TAX DEDUCTIBLE

Did you know if you pay for your child's tuition you can get it back (most of it) in taxes? Side note though: if your child used a fellowship, scholarship, or grant to pay for the tuition that is NOT deductible. However, if you used your own hard earned (or easy earned) money you can get it back in taxes. For more information on taxes Do your research (irs.gov) or you can read a book entitled: It's How Much You Keep That Counts! Not How Much You Make, by Robert R. Mueller, MBA, Ph.D. You can purchase the book at the following website: http://rabugary.mymobisite.us/getthebook

RAISE UP YOUR CHILD

This section might seem useless, but I felt the need to add due to an experience a classmate of mine had. So a classmate of mine told me when our school had an open house a parent asked her if the school had maids on campus. She replied no, and the parent responded with; then who will do my son's laundry? I could not believe my ears when I heard that.

Parents, please raise up your children. By the time they are in college they should know how to cook, clean, do laundry, basically take care of themselves. I mean you do want them to move out eventually, right? So then you should be teaching them little by little starting at; at least the age of 10. By the time they are 17/18/19 they should be independent of their parents when it comes to home economics. Don't wait for the school system to teach them. You gave birth to them it is your duty to teach them.

TO THE STUDENT

There are so many ways you can save or get money for college before and during college.

SCHOLARSHIPS AND GRANTS

The obvious, something everyone knows about, but very few do anything about. I will admit I could have done so much more to get a free ride to college. There are thousands maybe millions of scholarship all over the place. Free money for you to apply for. Yes its a lot of work, but it's better than having debt for the rest of your life. There are scholarships for everybody (lefties, males, females, Africans, Asians, Hispanics, Irish, disabled, writers, artists, athletes, mathematicians, scientists, Christians, Jews, film makers, photographers, short, tall, dancers, book readers, etc, etc, etc.). They have scholarships for anyone and everyone. Do your research and find them. Scholarships are usually given by organizations, companies, and schools whereas grants are mostly given by the government. Again they are out there you just have to find them. Below are a few websites where you can find scholarships and grants. There are much more you just have to search for it.

scholarships.com

studentscholarships.org

fastweb.com

unigo.com/scholarships

finaid.org/scholarships

collegescholarships.org

studentscholarshipsearch.com

internationalscholarships.com

scholars4dev.com

college-scholarships.com/free-scholarship-searches

scholarshipamerica.org

grants.gov

http://www.hesaa.org/Pages/NJGrantsHome.aspx

governmentgrant.com

grants.com

usagovernmentgrants.org/Government_Grants.html

WORK FOR IT

Yes, the old fashion way, work for it. You can legally get a job at 15. Get a job and save your money. Discipline yourself to not buy the latest gadgets or fashion and open a savings account and save, save, and save. If you're not 15 then freelance (baby-sit, shovel snow, cut grass, walk dogs, get a paper route, rake leaves, make and sell jewelry (or art), garage/yard sales, self-publish books, etc.) if you start young and get a savings account with good interest it adds up.

JOIN SOMETHING

Many organizations give money for college (churches, theatre companies, athletic groups, etc.) Join something of interest and be your best. Get involved and volunteer. This not only leads to a scholarship, but it could lead to a great job which you can use as not only money, but a reference. This may also be a place where you can intern for credit. It'll be great because it'll be something you enjoy doing so it won't be as difficult as writing essays to win a scholarship. This is also great for your college application.

RESEARCH FOR MORE OPTIONS

I am sure there are so many other options for saving money so you can go to college without getting a loan, but if you want more options as stated earlier you need to do your research. Books are NOT written to hide information from "a people", they are written to share information with people. It is up to "the people" to search and read it. As the good book says, ask and it shall be given, search and ye shall find." You have to search for it. "It" doesn't need you so it's not coming to you; you need "it" so you have to go to it.

WHY I AM COMPLETELY AGAINST FINANCIAL AID

First off, I went to college and did not get financial aid. My mother paid for it. I went to a county college and then transferred to a university and finished my schooling there. Both schools offered 3-4 payments for the semester. So she didn't have to pay it in full she had 3-4 months to complete the payment. If you are smart enough to start saving NOW you will have more than enough, and even if you don't have enough just as long as both child and parent are working you can use your savings to start and pay the rest with both of your pay checks. Once I got a job I began to make payments. They were minor, but I was still contributing. I am completely against financial aid because it should be illegal. School loans are the only loans in the universe that are NOT forgiven. You are better off getting a business loan and having your child start a business. Then at least he/she will be making money and can pay off the loan or at least have it forgiven within 7 years (see section two.) The only reason why the government is making a big deal about college is because of the money they make off of student loan debts. Many people die with their debt. That is not good. Their interests are the highest than any other loan (WHY IS THAT?) and they do not help you in any way to completely pay it off. So if you ask me never get a student loan for college. There are many other options (even more than this book offers. Do your research.) You just need to find them and do them.

CHOOSING A COLLEGE

Now that you have your money for college its time to choose a college. Again Research is needed. Depending on your major depends on your choice. For the MOST part the college you choose does not matter. Every college has its forte (for instance Kean University is the best college in NJ for a teacher's degree). However, no matter where you go they will teach you the basics, the rest you will learn on the job. So don't go crazy trying to get into an expensive or well-known college. Unless you saved for it don't go in debt for any college or university. It's not worth it. My first two years in college I went to a county college and a few of the professors were working part-time at the county (community) college and full-time at a prestige university. So I got the prestige university professor at the community college price. You can't beat that. If you know where you want to go figure out how much it will cost for six years (always have more than enough) and begin saving, however if you choose to go else where at least you'll have the money. Do not stress yourself out over college names. Once you go to that college you will realize none of that matters. The only reason people care about Ivy leagues is to impress people. If you haven't impressed yourself by now forget trying to impress people. It's never going to happen. Do your research, apply to at least to two schools (there is an application fee. Don't go into debt applying for college) and once you make your decision remember to continue saving money. Most importantly remember you are there for an EDUCATION. Not to party, get drunk, have sex, sexually assault people, do drugs, make friends, and/or pledge to be apart of a group. You are there for an education only. All the rest is not going to mean anything once you get out. It's a waste of time.

CHOOSING A MAJOR

This is the most difficult thing to do. I will tell you why. Not only me, but people I know went to college, graduated, and then became successful in a completely different field. The field they are working in now has nothing to do with their degree and they have chosen to NOT get a degree in the field they are in. So it's as if time and money was wasted. I honestly cannot help you in this field. The only thing I can say is start volunteering in the community (churches, food banks, theatre companies, thrift shops, sports leagues, girl/boy scouts, etc.) around the age of 13-18. In volunteering you will find gifts and talents you did not know you had. And in finding them you will more than likely find what you want to do (which will be different from what you thought you wanted to do prior to volunteering). I know this may sound wrong, but that's how I found out what I really wanted. Becoming an author and artist was something I came into the knowledge of due to volunteering in church. I went to college for theatre hoping to be a Tony Award winning Broadway actor, but now I don't care for that. I never knew back then that I would be an author and artist owning his own gift and art business. Had I paid more attention to what I was doing (that was helping people and not myself) I would have caught on earlier and changed my major. That's the other thing I need to mention. When you choose a major ask yourself the following question: "What job/work can I do that will benefit people before (if it does) it benefits me?" In other words choose a selfless major and not a selfish major. What you do needs to feed the hungry, heal the sick, give peace to the depressed, free people from their addictions, bring justice to those who have been done wrong, etc, etc, and etc. People in your community should benefit from what you are doing more than you benefit. Hopefully that helps you choose the right major. If not, don't worry, depending on what you choose to do you won't need a degree anyways (see section two for more details).

GET A JOB/WORK

Make sure you are working. Either get a job near home, the school, or get an on campus job. You will need finances for food, laundry, books, supplies, and so much more. You should not depend on daddy and/or mommy (or grandparents, aunts, uncles, etc.) for money. You should have your own for the basics.

MORE WAYS OF SAVING MONEY

Okay now you are in college and you still have to pay for supplies and food, etc. how do you save money? First and foremost I know you are annoyed with your parents you are ready to get far, far away, but when you go to a community college outside of your county or a university/college outside your state you have to pay more than those who live near by. So try your best to stay near home. If you still want to get away then be aware of that and save more money (in your savings account(s)) before going to college.

BOOKS: Never purchase books or supplies from the college bookstore (unless you cannot find it anywhere else.) Purchase your books used online. Even with shipping it's so much cheaper. Also check your school's library or local library and get the book for free. Using library books are great for English and literary classes (even theatre classes) because for the most part you only need the book for a certain amount of time. For instance let's say you're in class and you have to read Romeo and Juliet. Get the book from the library. Yes your page numbers will be different, but you can easily catch up (I did). For the most part you will be done with the book before the deadline to return it. If not simply extend the check out date (I did). Lastly check thrift shops, second hand shops, and garage/yard sales. You never know what they may have.

SUPPLIES: Dollar stores, yard/garage sales, thrift stores, listia.com, Ebay, etc. Or simply borrow it. Ask family, friends, strangers, even enemies if you can borrow, just make sure you return it as you received it.

COUPONS

You made fun of your mother for clipping those coupons, but now it's not such a bad idea. From food to laundry detergent to bathroom supplies coupons are awesome for saving. When it comes to food make sure you buy quality foods. I know we get the urge to buy cheap foods, but cheap foods are cheap for a reason (unhealthy and unsafe). You do not want to be worrying about your health while in college. But cheap clothing, shoes, pocketbooks, jewelry, paper towels, etc, but never put your health at risk. A great site to go to is sendearnings.com. There are many things you can do in this website (watch videos, surveys, fulfill offers, engine search, and more.), but I am telling you about this site because of the coupons. Once you sign up you go to the Deals section and click on coupons. Soon a bunch of coupons will appear (it takes about 5-10mins to view them all) and you click on the ones you want. At then end you click print and your printer will print them (you will have to cut them). You then take them to your store and use them. Within 3-5 weeks you earn $0.10 on each coupon you use. It sounds like a small amount, but four years of coupons add up. Plus there are other things you can do to gain money. Once you make $40 you can request a check (There's a fee (which they take out of your check) once you request them to send it). Not bad.

OBEY THE SCHOOL'S RULES

From parking to dorm rules, obey the rules. It may be a small amount, but getting a parking ticket, or fee for going against the rules is still money wasted. Behave yourself and save yourself and money. Also you would hate to be asked to leave the school. That basically goes on your permanent record and it is difficult to get into another school or a get job because of it. So again behave yourself. Trying to fit in with the crowd, or violating parking, or anything else is not worth the trouble or money.

PASS THE CLASS

In college C is the lowest you can get to pass the class. If you get a D or F you have to take the class again (you do not get credits for Ds and Fs.) Yes you can take it again, but you also have to pay for it again. Again that is money wasted. So pass it the first time. Discipline yourself and prioritize your time to do what is needed to pass. If you are having problems speak to the professor or get a tutor (most colleges (if not all) have free tutoring services, do your research on that. If they don't have one than create one.

GO TO A WORK COLLEGE

There are only seven work colleges in America, so this idea is limited, but it's nice to know you have the option. Basically you work and in your work you either are assisted in paying tuition or do not have to pay at all. Hopefully more of these will begin to pop up. For more information on work colleges go to: http://www.workcolleges.org/

CREDIT SHARKS

Run; fly if you have to, away from the credit card people. It is completely awful that colleges allow these people on the campus. Who are "these people?" Credit card companies hire people (usually college students) to go to colleges to get college students to get credit cards. Simply because they (credit card companies) know that college students are desperate for money and are too ignorant to read the fine print. The interest rates are usually too high and by the time you sign on the dotted line and realize what you have done you are now in debt (or double debt if you applied for a student loan). As soon as they (credit sharks) come to you run, run, and run some more.

INTERN, INTERN, INTERN

Internships are the best thing a college student could/should do. Spring, summer, autumn, and winter, you need to intern every semester. Even if you are not taking classes you need to intern. Internships bring you contacts, references, experience, credits, and most importantly possible jobs or career opportunities. And don't box yourself in with your internships. Take an internship outside your major, it very well can lead you to a love/passion you didn't know you had.

INTERVIEWS

Whether an internship or job interview there is a few things you should know. First: NEVER BE LATE. I don't care if there are horses falling from the moon trying to make you late. Find a way to fight off those horses to make sure you are EARLY. Not on time, but early. Your arrival is the first thing that determines whether or not you get the internship/job. Fifteen to thirty minutes early is the standard. Secondly, look presentable. First impressions are everything. Look like you care. Gentlemen wear slacks or dressed pants (PULL YOUR PANTS UP. The interviewer does not need or want to see your underwear.), tucked in dressed shirt and tie. If you do not know how to tie a tie go to youtube there are hundreds of tutorials. Ladies: you don't need to dress like a nun, but don't dress like a prostitute either. Nothing too tight and nothing hanging out. Wearing too revealing clothes will either make the interviewer uninterested in you or interested in you for the wrong reasons. Dress for success. Third: research a little something about the company. Know their mission statement and even use it in your answers. For instance when they ask you why you want to work here, if their mission statement is "To bring great service to those in need with care" Then you can say something like: "I would like to provide great service to your customers with much care." This way the interviewer knows you did your research on the company (they like that). Fourth: know something about yourself. Every interviewer asks that annoying question. Don't mention your personal life, but your business life. They want to know your past experience in the field, why you're interested in the field, and the time span you have been in the field. RESEARCH for how to succeed an interview or job interview books.

THAT'S IT

Well that's all the college advice I can think of at the moment. If I think of more I will update this book. But as of now for those choosing college this all you need to get started. Stay focused, ask questions (Even the stupid ones), but most of all do your research. Mistakes are made (for the most part) because someone believed what they heard and they made bad choices through ignorance. Therefore, if you research you will make a lot less mistakes than those who just believe what they are told. Again, evaluate your life and see if college is necessary (for most people it is NOT.)

NOT TO COLLEGE

So many people are under the wrong impression (the lie) that college is the only road to success. It is not the only road it is one road and not the best road (depending on your profession). This section of the book will give you your options that have always existed, but because you refused to research you didn't know (I hope you're getting the point of the importance of research). As said earlier education is NOT expensive, college is expensive, but only one type of education NOT the only. You will now see your many different options, which again depending on what you want to do are much better options than college.

TRADE SCHOOL

Trade schools offer training in a specific training in a wide variety of skilled careers. The cool thing about these schools is they don't waste your time teaching you a bunch of stuff you will never use at work. They won't ask you when Peter and Paul will be meeting Jesus by the rock depending on the time, location, mileage, and kilometers, they began they're travels. If it's not needed to complete your work you won't learn it. And because it will be your interest you will enjoy it (yeah they'll be some cons, but they won't outweigh the pros. Besides every job has its cons. Nothing is perfect.) You also have a better chance of getting work once you are done and you'll only spend any where from a year to two in training. Some of these careers include:

Construction, Welding, Carpentry, Landscaping, Heating, Ventilation, and Air Conditioning Technician, Brick Mason, Elevator Installer and Repairer, Mechanics, Electrical, Painting (Buildings, Homes, etc), Forestry, Photography, Woodworking, Masonry, Locksmithing, Metal Work, Child care, Chef, and so much more. There is a much longer list at the following website:

http://www.theworkingcentre.org/types-trades/393

If you know for sure you are interested in any one of these fields than do your research on the closest trade school and apply.

JOIN THE MILITARY

I am against this idea (it's not for me), but my goal is to give you your options and then you decide what you want. There is the ROTC program, but also ,the Army, Marine Corps, Navy, Air Force, and Coast Guard. Do your research. There is Active Duty (Full Time), Reserve (Part Time), and National Guard (Part Time). For more information, visit the following websites:

www.military.com

www.todaysmilitary.com

NETWORK MARKETING

Many people call this pyramid schemes, but they are not. There are many credible companies and people succeeding from network marketing. Basically a company sells a product and their associates are their advertising. Meaning instead of using their profits to make commercials, newspapers/magazines ads, and/or billboards they use their profits to pay people (associates). There are many companies and more on the way. The best way to be successful is find a company that offers a need that not only you need, but you are willing to share with others (Make sure you see the statement after the conclusion). Just to get you started here are a few network marketing companies: LegalShield, Avon, Amway, Melaleuca, Organo Gold, 5Linx, Youngevity, MaryKay, Young Living Essential Oils, Shaklee, and ID Life. For more you can visit: http://www.nexera.com/top25/ and don't forget RESEARCH.

BECOME AN APPRENTICE

The idea of being an apprentice is older than the television show of the same name. The idea of an apprentice started in the late middle ages (1300-1500). Basically you assist a professional or skilled employer (they train you) for a period of time and they pay you (pay is not great, but it can lead to greater things (depending on what you do with what you learn)). Again do your research. To help you out just a little below are some companies that offer apprenticeship: Enstitute, Echoing Green, TechStars, UnCollege Gap Year (Tuition Based), Thiel Fellowship.

There are much more. Go search and ye shall find.

ONLINE CLASSES

There are online classes that give you great information you can use. Some of these websites also offer certification, which is great for your resume. For the most part, now-a-days, employers just want to know you know something. They don't care how you know it, just that you know it. Some websites are: Coursera, Udacity, Khan Academy, Alison, Udemy, EdX, Uncollege, and so much more (do your research.) Some are free, and others you have to pay, but it's not as expensive as college (proving not all education is expensive.). I would combine this with volunteering. Volunteering and certifications on your resume is a plus in getting the job.

ADULT EDUCATION

Adult/Continuing education is courses offered by high schools or county/community schools. There are fees, but not as expensive as college. Basically you take courses specific to the work/job/career you want and they most times offer certification (If not you can still post on your resume which classes you took and where). They give you the knowledge, information, and education you need to work in which ever field. The fields range from graphic design to fitness to carpentry to arts to massage therapy, and so many more. Simply go to your local public high school, vocational school, or community/county College and they will happily give you information (brochure or catalog) on the courses and fees.

VOLUNTEER

This next idea is for those who do not know what you want to do with your life. You know your parent's want you to go to college, but you have no clue what your major should be. NEVER GO TO COLLEGE WITHOUT KNOWING YOUR MAJOR. You're only going to waste time and money. You can hook up with Peace Corps or AmeriCorp. As said earlier you can also volunteer at your church, thrift store, or any tax exempt organization. Other organizations include: Habitat for Humanity, YMCA, Big Brothers Big Sisters of America, Corporation for National Community Service, Boy/Girl Scouts, Boys and Girls Clubs of America, National Park Services, and so much more. Do your research. Again volunteering is great for the resume and it will help identify what you do well and what you enjoy doing.

GET A JOB

There are many jobs that do not require a college degree. And that job could lead to a life long career. With promotions you can start out as an associate and end up the general manager or even an owner of a franchise. It has happened many times in America, so it is possible. It takes time and patience (all good things do), but it is still possible. You can also go to career fairs. Even without a college degree you can receive a good job at a career fair. Especially if you have a good resume with certifications and volunteering (we discussed those things already. I hope you remember)

TRAVEL

If you were smart enough to save for college or your parent's were then you have the money. Take a year off from schooling (right after high school) and travel. Either in your country (from state to state) or outside (you'll need a passport) from country to country. Not only will you see and experience things, people, and places that you have never experienced before, new ideas and insight will come your way. All of these things can tell you what you want to do whether its college or another option even an option that is not in this book. Traveling is something all people should do. You have a small perception of life by staying in your area. There is so much out there (ideas, views, creations, inventions, and more) that you don't even know exists and in traveling you could bring an idea back home that could cause you to be very successful without that college degree. Or traveling could cause you to see what you really need to do and you will choose the correct degree and you can spend your time wisely in college. Besides, I do not believe anyone should go to college after high school. Science tells us that our brains are not fully functional until we hit the age of 21. So then why are we asking our children to make an important life decision at the age of 18? That is ignorance and doesn't make any sense. We should give them their time to realize why they are here, what problems they are here to solve and then make that decision. They should live life before choosing a life decision (that could either break or make you).

BECOME A SUPERHERO

Well not a superhero, but a hero. Police officers, firemen, and EMTs do not need a degree. They have academies of their own where they train you. Firemen/women as well as EMT's for the most part start out as volunteers and can be promoted to paid positions. Police officers go through boot camp (not all men/women make it through.) There's not only paper testing, but physical testing. You have to past all in order to become a police officer. To be a detective or a higher position (CIA, FBI, etc) you need a college degree, however, you may be able to go to a vocational or trade school and get certified for one of those positions. Do your research on what is needed and then make a choice.

FOLLOW JESUS

If you want to work as a chaplain, missionary, pastor, clergymen/women or any other field in faith than you don't need college. However there are seminaries as well as faith based schools specifically for these fields. The thing about this is you do not waste your time in classes you do not need. (You still won't have to figure out when Peter and Paul are meeting Jesus by the rock.) You will only be taking classes needed in your field and you will also have field work so you can get a taste of the job before taking the job. Do your research. There are many schools, seminaries, and now churches that are certified and offer degrees as well as certifications for these types of fields.

LIE, CHEAT, AND STEAL

Become a politician. This is a joke, please do NOT be offended. But seriously you do not need to have a degree to be a politician. The requirements are as followed:

If you want to be a Senator you have to be at least 30 years old, a U.S. citizen for at least nine years at the time of election to the Senate, and a resident of the state one is elected to represent in the Senate. If you want to be a Representative you have to be at least 25 years old, a citizen of the United States for at least seven years prior to election and a resident of the state he or she is chosen to represent. To become a mayor you need to be US Citizen, are a legal adult (18 or older), and you must be permanent resident of the city/town you are running for. There may be some other requirements, but they vary by city/town. Do your research. To be a governor varies from state to state. Generally you have to be a certain age (varies), be a U.S. citizen, and lived in the state for a certain amount of years (depending on the state 5-10 years). If you want to be the President according to law (which by now you should know means nothing depending on who you know) you simply have to have been born in America, be at least 35 years of age and have lived in the United States for at least 14 years. (Meaning if you were born in America, but then moved out of the country, when you return to the states, you need to have been a citizen for 14+ years). The only other thing you need is lots of money for campaigning, which if you were saving money for college like section one talks about than you should have enough. If not you can always accept bribes. Okay, sorry if you were offended by that. For more information visit:

http://usgovinfo.about.com/

VOCATIONAL/SPECIALTY SCHOOLS

Just like trade schools specialty schools only train you in the specific job you are training for. No useless unnecessary classes or studies. This is great because again you only spend six months to about year in training and you learn only what you need to know. These types of jobs/careers include: Salon/Barber/Cosmetology, Health Care/Medical Assistants/Aids, Real Estate Agents, Insurance Brokers, Chefs/Culinary Arts, Truck Driving, Welding, Business/Marketing Management, Electronics, Automotive Technology, Massage Therapist, Pharmacy Technician, Computer Programmers, and Paralegals.

Of course there are so much more. Do your research. Again these options cost a lot less money and you spend a lot less time in training and you get to get right to work. And the cool thing is in most of these you can start your own business. Which brings me to the next option (my favorite).

BE YOUR OWN BOSS

This area is the largest option. And now-a-days with the internet it is so much easier. There are many titles for people who take this option which are: Freelancer, Entrepreneur, Independent Contractor, Consultant, Business Owner, Sole Proprietor, Contingency worker, Open-Collar worker, Free agent, and so much more. Basically you either go into business for yourself or you start a business and create jobs. The great thing about this is you can do this in just about any field.

ATHLETICS: You don't have to have a degree. You can either go to a trade or vocational school. When it comes to playing sports you can try-out for minor leagues and work your way up. Or for things like track do 5K runs and once you are noticed you can easily make a living.

ARTS: Performing, Graphic, or Fine Arts it is so much easier (but still a lot of work, time, money, and consistency) than ever before to work for yourself. You can produce your own albums, own shows, own galleries, you name it, it can all be done. Do your research and find other freelancers and ask questions.

AUTHOR: Self-Publishing gets easier each year and finding other freelancers to help (editors, graphic designers, marketers, publicists, etc.) is easier and most times are affordable (Check out fiverr.com for affordable freelancers).

HOBBYIST: Why just have a hobby. Whether baking, crocheting, fixing things around the house, cooking, blogging, collecting items, and whatever else. You can turn that into a business.

GAMER: Play games and master them. Then find contests and enter them. Most of them offer big money prizes. Soon you can be sponsored by a big company.

LEARN A LANGUAGE: Learn another language (really well) and become a freelance translator. You'll make a lot in that because translators are needed. Not to mention it looks good on your resume that you speak another language.

STORE OWNER: There is always something that your town doesn't have that is needed. Instead driving over to the next town or exit (if you live in Jersey), why not help out the community by starting a business that offers what they need, but cannot get in town. Fulfill a need. Whatever that need may be, fulfill it. Or even fulfill a want. A video arcade, a specialty restaurant, an odds and end store with goodies you can get no where else. Yes it's a lot of work, but you don't have to knock on interviewer's door just to get work. As per money, well you were going to get a student loan why not get a business loan instead. The interests are lower and easier to pay off. Do your research. There are many books in the library (free education) about starting a business, getting loans, freelancing, marketing, etc, etc, etc. Find them, read them, take notes, and ask questions. There are many groups and organizations (Research to find them.) that have meetings to help other freelancers/entrepreneurs to be successful.

Which brings me to my last suggestion which goes along with starting your own business.

But before I go there know that there are so many other jobs you can do on your own. Basically there are many tasks out there that people cannot do nor want to do and are willing to pay someone to do it. There are many websites where you can find work as a freelancer. Find them. Here are some: Freelancer.com; freelance.com; guru.com; fiverr.com; ifreelance.com; upwork.com; gigbux.com; and so much more. A great book to read on freelancing is *The Complete Idiot's Guide to Making Money in Freelancing* by Laurie E. Rozakis, Ph.D. Don't be offended by the title, you're not an idiot it just means you do not need a rocket science degree to understand it. There is so much more, in fact there are books dedicated to this topic. Go to the library and search freelance, entrepreneur, and start a business. You will find so (maybe too) many books you can learn from (all free). Lastly, know that this is the original way people worked. There were no jobs. Every family had their own businesses and it was automatically willed down to the oldest living child once the parents died. There were no bosses or CEOs, no college, no degrees, none of that existed. Your parent's taught you the business and you taught your children, and they taught their children, and so on.

Okay time to get to the last option.

ATTEND WORKSHOPS

Expos, conferences, conventions, festivals, workshops, classes, seminars, and so much more are offered every day. Not only do you get great information (even information you don't get from college) it is great for networking. Where you can either find your next job that can lead to your career or you can get possible customers (if you are starting a business). Again you have to RESEARCH: How to start a business seminar, real estate workshops, art festivals, and so many other options. Again you receive education (not free, but not expensive. There is a registration fee, but is worth the money. Fee varies) and contacts. These types of events are produced and taught by people and professionals already in the business with experience and life lessons they are eager to share with you. And usually at the end of the class they open the floor for questions and answers. So if there is anything you don't understand you can ask. And in most cases the teacher/professional usually makes time for one on one talk after the class is over. This also can be added to your resume. There are also stores that offer classes for instance art stores offers art classes, music stores offer music lessons, and home improvement stores offer classes on home improvement. The classes relatively inexpensive and your teacher is someone who works in the business. Again this is great for a resume and you only learn what you need to know.

CONCLUSION

This may not be the end and there maybe hundreds more options and even more to come, but now that's all I have to share. Of course if none of these options fit you either it's time for you to do your research or it's time for you to stop being lazy. In the end you are a unique individual with your own unique fingerprints. Do not just do what everyone else is doing. Not only research your options, but research yourself. Figure out what makes you angry, or sad, and find a solution. Think about all the things you wish existed and create them. Figure out what you feel needs to be fixed and fix them. Through it all you will find you, your gifts/talents, your calling, and of course your career. You will enjoy it even the annoying parts, and learn and most importantly you will be helping and assisting people, not just existing (which is what most people do). So get out there and find you and not some carbon copy of you. You are not an average person so stop thinking like an average person. If you wouldn't jump off a bridge, or jump in a lake (if you cannot swim), or stand in the middle of a busy highway simply because everyone else is doing it, then do not got to college just to get job with a student loan just because everyone else is doing it. There are always options you just need to do your research. Knock, search, and ask. I hope this book assisted you in your endeavors if not I apologize for wasting your time. I wish you well and have an awesome time researching.

FINAL THOUGHTS

There are three things I would like to leave with you. First, what is success?

Most people believe success is making billions of dollars so they can buy a mansion with a staff, expensive cars, and splurge, splurge, and splurge some more. That is 100% wrong. Successful people are solving problems. Helping people and being selfless. Pretty much if you want to make money: help people. Feed the hungry, heal the sick, house the homeless, save the abused children, help people find their missing sock, etc. Be or create a solution to people's problems. That is what success is. Thinking about someone else's problems and helping them solve them. Fix things that are broken, whether it be hearts or televisions. Be the one who makes the world, or your country, state, or city or better place to live. When you have other people in mind instead of your selfish self than you will be successful. Second thought: Success can never come from a microwave. There are a few things you need to have, they need to be strong in order to receive complete success, and that is consistency, compassion, patience, faith, discipline, and a positive attitude. No success is overnight. You need to know that the best and healthiest things take time, money, and patience. Quick, fast, cheap, and easy lead to nowhere good quickly. If you want the best you have to know it comes in time and you need to be faithful and consistent in all you do. Third and last, there is no such thing as failures or mistakes in business/success. They are lessons learned. The best ideas, inventions, and creativity came/comes from failure. It causes you to think higher and better, and causes you to think differently. Failure causes you to think of things that brings success. These things you would have never thought of had you not "failed." So never be disappointed in failure. Allow it to motivate you to keep going. Success comes from an oven. Yes it takes longer, but it lasts for eternity (and it's healthier). Your success cooked in an oven (as opposed to a microwave) will last beyond you.

If you do things right your success will be handed down to your children, grandchildren, great grandchildren, etc, etc, and etc. In the 1890s Lewis Latimer invented the light bulb that we still use today (Thomas Edison's light bulb only lasted a few days and is not the one we use today). That's what can happen when your goal is not money, money, money, and it is help, help, help. You can create something that will last forever. So remember this while you go to college, or start a business, or go to trade school, or follow Jesus, or (you get the point), remember to ask yourself two questions: Who can I help and how can I help them? And if you are still in high school or middle school start asking it now. Think of something(s) that really bothers you. Something(s) that makes you angry, something(s) you wish someone would fix, a problem you want solved, a matter you wish someone would take in their hands and make it better. All of those wishes you need to take them and do something about them. And you know what you don't have to wait until you go to college. No matter how old you are (while reading this book), 15, 25, or 105 you can begin to think about how you can solve that problem and begin to solve it NOW. You will become successful in solving that problem. I hope you received much knowledge and wisdom from this book and hope you decide to be the unique you and become that problem solver you were created to be.

SOURCES USED FOR INFORMATION

Jeremy Anderberg, The Art of Manliness, April 17, 2014,

website,

http://www.artofmanliness.com/2014/04/17/is-college-for-

everyone-10-alternatives-to-the-traditional-4-year-college/

Lindsay Hutton, Family Education, FEN Learning, website,

http://life.familyeducation.com/slideshow/teen/65778.html?p

age=9

James Altucher, Slideshare.net, Linkedin, May 25, 2014,

website,

http://www.slideshare.net/JamesAltucher/james-altucher-40-

alternatives-to-college/01-

WRITE_AND_PITCH_YOUR_OWN_TV_SHOW

SUGGESTED READING

Author Dave Ramsey

Read anything this author has written, but specifically

"The Total Money Makeover."

If you want to be wealthy and make better choices with your

money, you need to read this book. *Thank you, Valerie Moses.*

UPDATE

I just found out that there are ways to forgive the student loan (if you should have one). Therefore, I figure I add this to the book. There are many so do your research. Some only allow you to lower the interest rate so you can ay it off sooner, but I am only sharing how to completely cancel it. These are the top three ways. Again, there are more, simply do your research. You will be amazed of how much you do NOT know simply because you refuse to research beyond what you are being taught.

1. Become a public school teacher in a low-income area.

2. Join the military.

3. Get a public service, government, or non-profit job.

There are companies that help you cancel the debt, but that cost money so study and do it yourself. It takes time and patience, but at least you know that is debt you will no longer have.

TITLES BY CASEY BELL

The Diary of Stephanie Dane

4Score

Crystal Fountain

Buried Lies, Surface

The House on Atticus Lane

Moving 4Ward

Essays From Dysfunctional Families: Literary Betrayal

A Family of Strangers

CHILDREN'S BOOKS

You Are Beautiful

How To Love Your Bully

The Day the Rainbow Broke Up

http://authorcaseybell.weebly.com/

http://payhip.com/caseysbell

bookcasepublishing.weebly.com